Disclaimer

The information in this book, "Predict Altcoin Season Run: Unlock the Bitcoin Dominance Code," is for educational purposes only and does not constitute financial, investment, or trading advice. Cryptocurrency investments, including Bitcoin, altcoins, and memecoins, are highly speculative and carry substantial risk. The value of cryptocurrencies can be extremely volatile and may result in significant financial loss.

The author and publisher do not endorse, support, or guarantee the accuracy or reliability of any information, projects, or investments discussed in this book.

The mention of specific cryptocurrencies, blockchain projects, developers, or tokens is not an endorsement. Readers should be aware of the potential for market manipulation, fraud, and the inherent risks associated with blockchain technology and cryptocurrency investments.

The author and publisher disclaim any liability for any loss or damage incurred as a result of reliance on the information in this book. Readers are solely responsible for their own investment decisions and should carefully consider the risks before investing in any cryptocurrency.

By reading this book, you agree to the terms of this disclaimer

Copyright ©Dwatne Anderson   2024

Table of Contents

Foreword
Introduction
Chapter 1: Demystifying Altcoins
Chapter 2: Understanding Bitcoin Dominance
Chapter 3: The Impact of Bitcoin Dominance on Altcoins
Chapter 4: Key Indicators and Metrics for Altcoin Analysis
Chapter 5: The Dance of Dominance: How Bitcoin Impacts Altcoin Seasons
Chapter 6: Predicting Altcoin Bull Runs
Chapter 7: Investing Strategies for Altcoins
Chapter 8: The Future of Bitcoin and Altcoins
Chapter 9: Chapter 9: Top Ranking Altcoins and Memecoins
Chapter 10 : Conclusion
Appendices
Glossary of Key Terms

Foreword

Welcome to a journey through the dynamic and often unpredictable world of cryptocurrencies.

This book, "Predict Altcoin Season Run: Unlock the Bitcoin Dominance Code," is designed to guide both novice and seasoned investors through the intricacies of Bitcoin dominance and its profound impact on the broader cryptocurrency market.

Here, you will discover the pivotal moments and market conditions that herald the lucrative phases of altcoin bull runs.

Through these pages, we aim to demystify the complex interplay between Bitcoin and altcoins, providing you with the knowledge and strategies to navigate the market with confidence and insight.

Introduction

Cryptocurrencies have revolutionized the financial landscape, offering a decentralized alternative to traditional banking systems.

While Bitcoin remains the most well-known cryptocurrency, thousands of other digital assets, known as altcoins, have emerged. Understanding the interplay between Bitcoin and altcoins is crucial for navigating the complex cryptocurrency market.

This book delves into the intricacies of Bitcoin dominance and altcoin seasons and provides data-driven strategies for maximizing gains in the cryptocurrency market.

The journey of cryptocurrencies began over a decade ago with the inception of Bitcoin, which introduced the world to the possibility of digital currencies operated by decentralized consensus rather than a central authority.

As Bitcoin gained prominence and acceptance, it paved the way for numerous other cryptocurrencies, collectively known as altcoins, that sought to improve upon or offer different uses than Bitcoin.

This book, "Predict Altcoin Season Run: Unlock the Bitcoin Dominance Code," explores the dynamic relationship between Bitcoin and altcoins, focusing on how changes in Bitcoin's market dominance can herald lucrative altcoin seasons.

An altcoin season, or 'altseason,' refers to periods where altcoins significantly outperform Bitcoin in terms of price gains. Understanding these seasons and the factors that predict their onset is crucial for investors looking to maximize their returns in the cryptocurrency market.

A Brief History of Altcoin Seasons
The term "altcoin season" refers to periods when altcoins outperform Bitcoin significantly.

Historically, these seasons have been triggered by various factors, including technological advancements, market sentiment shifts, and regulatory changes. For instance, the altcoin season of 2017 saw unprecedented growth in the value of many altcoins, driven by the ICO (Initial Coin Offering) boom.

Understanding these historical patterns can provide valuable insights into future market movements.

The history of altcoin seasons is intricately linked to Bitcoin's market cycles. Historically, altcoin seasons have often followed massive rallies in Bitcoin's price when investors started to diversify their gains into riskier assets.

For instance, notable altcoin seasons in late 2017 and early 2021 saw many altcoins achieve all-time highs shortly after Bitcoin reached peak prices. T
These seasons are characterized by a decrease in Bitcoin's dominance index—a metric that measures Bitcoin's market capitalization relative to the total market cap of all cryptocurrencies.

When this index declines, it often indicates that money is flowing into altcoins at a higher rate than into Bitcoin.

Throughout this book, we'll delve into the indicators and market dynamics that can help predict the onset of altseasons.

We'll explore various technical, economic, and sentiment-driven indicators that have historically correlated with the shifting tides of investment from Bitcoin to altcoins.

By understanding these patterns, investors can position themselves to capitalize on the cyclical nature of the crypto market, potentially reaping substantial gains during these vibrant and exhilarating phases of the market.

As we proceed, the book will guide you through the complexities of cryptocurrency investments, from understanding basic concepts to applying advanced trading strategies.

Our goal is to equip you with the knowledge and tools needed to navigate the volatile waters of the crypto market with confidence and foresight.

Chapter 1: Demystifying Altcoins

Cryptocurrencies have revolutionized the financial landscape, offering a decentralized alternative to traditional banking systems. While Bitcoin remains the most well-known cryptocurrency, thousands of other digital assets, known as altcoins, have emerged. This chapter aims to demystify altcoins, providing an overview of their types, significance, and role in the cryptocurrency ecosystem.

Unveiling the World of Altcoins

Altcoins, short for "alternative coins," refer to all cryptocurrencies other than Bitcoin. Each altcoin operates on its own blockchain or as a token on another blockchain, providing unique features and functionalities. The diversity of altcoins reflects the growing innovation and experimentation within the cryptocurrency space.

The emergence of altcoins began shortly after Bitcoin's introduction in 2009.

Developers recognized that while Bitcoin was groundbreaking, it had limitations and lacked certain features. This realization led to the creation of new digital currencies that aimed to address these shortcomings or provide new functionalities. Litecoin, created in 2011, was one of the first altcoins and was designed to offer faster transaction times and a different hashing algorithm.

Types of Altcoins

Altcoins can be categorized into several types based on their functionality and underlying technology. Here are some of the most common types:

Utility Tokens: These tokens are used to access a specific product or service within a blockchain ecosystem. Examples include Ethereum (ETH) and Binance Coin (BNB). Ethereum, for instance, allows developers to build and deploy decentralized applications (dApps) on its platform.

BNB, originally launched as an ERC-20 token on Ethereum, now operates on Binance's own blockchain, Binance Chain, and is used for transaction fees on the Binance Exchange, among other uses.

Security Tokens: These represent ownership in a real-world asset, such as shares in a company or real estate. Security tokens are subject to regulatory scrutiny and must comply with securities laws.

An example is tZERO,(TZROP) which offers tokens that represent shares in its company, providing dividends to token holders.

Stablecoins: These are designed to maintain a stable value by being pegged to a fiat currency, commodity, or other assets. Tether (USDT) and USD Coin (USDC) are popular stablecoins.

They provide the benefits of cryptocurrency— such as quick transactions and security— without the price volatility typically associated with cryptocurrencies.

Privacy Coins: These focus on providing enhanced privacy and anonymity for transactions. Monero (XMR) and Zcash (ZEC) are examples of privacy coins.
Monero uses advanced cryptographic techniques to obscure transaction details, making it very difficult to trace transactions back to individuals. Zcash offers optional privacy features, allowing users to choose between transparent and shielded transactions.

Governance Tokens: These give holders the right to vote on decisions within a blockchain project. Examples include Maker (MKR) and Compound (COMP). MKR holders can vote on decisions affecting the MakerDAO ecosystem, such as changes to the DAI stablecoin system. COMP holders can vote on proposals to adjust parameters of the Compound protocol, which is a decentralized lending platform.

Importance of Altcoins in the Crypto Ecosystem

Altcoins play a crucial role in the cryptocurrency ecosystem by driving innovation and offering diverse investment opportunities.

They often introduce new features and functionalities that improve upon or differ from those of Bitcoin.

For example, Ethereum's smart contract capabilities have revolutionized the development of decentralized applications (dApps) and the entire decentralized finance (DeFi) sector.

Driving Innovation

One of the key contributions of altcoins is the introduction of new technologies and solutions that push the boundaries of what is possible with blockchain. Ethereum's smart contracts, for example, enable automated, self-executing agreements that do not require intermediaries.

This innovation has paved the way for DeFi, a rapidly growing sector that aims to recreate traditional financial systems—such as lending, borrowing, and trading—using blockchain technology.

Another example is Chainlink (LINK), which provides decentralized oracles to bring real-world data into smart contracts.
This capability is essential for many blockchain applications that require data from the outside world, such as weather information for insurance contracts or price feeds for decentralized exchanges.

Offering Diversification

Moreover, altcoins contribute to the overall growth and maturity of the cryptocurrency market. By offering various use cases and addressing different market needs, altcoins attract a broader range of investors and users.

This diversification helps to mitigate the risks associated with investing in a single cryptocurrency. For instance, while Bitcoin might be seen as a store of value similar to digital gold, altcoins like Ethereum can be seen as a platform for building decentralized applications.

Investors can also diversify their portfolios by investing in different types of altcoins, each with its own risk-reward profile. Stablecoins provide a safe harbor during times of market volatility, privacy coins offer anonymity, and utility tokens can provide access to valuable services and platforms.

Market Impact

Altcoins also play a significant role in shaping the market dynamics. For instance, during altcoin seasons, the price performance of altcoins can influence overall market sentiment and attract new investors.

Altcoin seasons occur when altcoins outperform Bitcoin, often leading to increased trading volumes and market activity.

Additionally, the development and adoption of altcoins can drive technological advancements and infrastructure improvements in the cryptocurrency ecosystem. As projects innovate and compete, they contribute to the robustness and resilience of the entire market.

Challenges and Risks

While altcoins offer numerous opportunities, they also come with challenges and risks. The altcoin market is highly volatile, and many projects fail to achieve their goals. Investors must conduct thorough research and due diligence before investing in altcoins.

Regulatory risks are also a concern, as governments around the world are still developing frameworks for cryptocurrency regulation. Security tokens, for instance, must comply with securities laws, which can vary significantly between jurisdictions.

Moreover, some altcoins may lack liquidity, making it difficult to buy or sell large amounts without affecting the price. Investors should be aware of these risks and consider them when making investment decisions.

In conclusion, altcoins are an integral part of the cryptocurrency ecosystem. Understanding their types, significance, and role is essential for any investor looking to navigate the dynamic and rapidly evolving world of digital assets.

Altcoins drive innovation, offer diversification, and play a critical role in market dynamics. However, they also come with risks that investors must carefully consider.

As we proceed to the next chapter, we will delve into the concept of Bitcoin dominance and its implications for the cryptocurrency market.
By understanding the interplay between Bitcoin and altcoins, investors can make more informed decisions and capitalize on the opportunities presented by this exciting and transformative technology.

Chapter 2: Understanding Bitcoin Dominance

As the progenitor of the cryptocurrency movement, Bitcoin not only introduced the world to blockchain technology but also set a benchmark for evaluating the health and trajectory of the broader crypto market.

One of the key metrics that helps investors gauge the market landscape is Bitcoin dominance.

Exploring Bitcoin Dominance

Bitcoin dominance measures Bitcoin's market capitalization relative to the total market capitalization of all cryptocurrencies combined.

This metric is crucial as it provides insights into the capital allocation within the crypto market, indicating whether investors are favoring Bitcoin over altcoins or diversifying their investments across a broader spectrum of digital assets.

The concept of Bitcoin dominance emerged as the cryptocurrency market expanded beyond Bitcoin. Initially, Bitcoin was almost synonymous with cryptocurrency, but the proliferation of altcoins introduced a need to understand Bitcoin's position relative to these new entrants.

Bitcoin dominance offers a snapshot of how market participants allocate their funds, highlighting periods of confidence or skepticism towards altcoins.

Calculation of Bitcoin Dominance
The formula for calculating Bitcoin dominance is straightforward:

How Bitcoin Dominance is Calculated

Bitcoin dominance is calculated using the following formula:

$$\text{Bitcoin Dominance (\%)} = \left(\frac{\text{Market Cap of Bitcoin}}{\text{Total Market Cap of All Cryptocurrencies}}\right) \times 100$$

For example, if the total market capitalization of all cryptocurrencies is $1 trillion and Bitcoin's market capitalization is $300 billion, Bitcoin dominance would be:

$$\text{Bitcoin Dominance (\%)} = \left(\frac{300 \text{ billion}}{1 \text{ trillion}}\right) \times 100 = 30\%$$

This metric is vital for understanding the money flow in the cryptocurrency market, as it helps investors gauge whether capital is flowing into Bitcoin or altcoins.

Historical Trends and Insights

Over the years, Bitcoin dominance has seen significant fluctuations. During Bitcoin's early years, it enjoyed nearly unchallenged dominance, accounting for over 90% of the total market cap.

However, as the market matured and more sophisticated and varied altcoins entered the market, Bitcoin's dominance began to waver.

Notable dips in Bitcoin dominance often correspond with altcoin rallies, particularly during periods known as 'altseasons,' where the value of altcoins rise dramatically compared to Bitcoin.

Bitcoin's Early Dominance

In the early days of cryptocurrency, Bitcoin was virtually synonymous with the entire market. The lack of viable alternatives meant that

Bitcoin's dominance was almost absolute, often exceeding 90%. This period, roughly from 2009 to 2013, was characterized by Bitcoin's clear leadership in market cap, technological development, and adoption.

The Rise of Altcoins

The introduction of Ethereum in 2015 marked a significant shift in the market.
Ethereum's smart contract functionality opened new possibilities, leading to the creation of numerous tokens and decentralized applications (dApps).

As a result, Bitcoin's dominance began to decline, dropping below 80% as investors started diversifying into Ethereum and other emerging altcoins.

Altseasons and Fluctuations

The term 'altseason' refers to periods when altcoins significantly outperform Bitcoin. These periods are typically marked by a decrease in Bitcoin dominance.

For instance, during the ICO boom of 2017, Bitcoin dominance fell to around 35% as investors flocked to new projects promising high returns. Similarly, in the first half of 2021, Bitcoin dominance dropped below 50% amidst a surge in interest in DeFi and NFTs.

The Impact of Bitcoin Dominance

Understanding Bitcoin dominance is vital for several reasons:

Market Sentiment

High Bitcoin dominance often indicates a risk-averse sentiment in the market, where investors prefer the relative safety of Bitcoin over the potentially higher but riskier returns of altcoins.

Conversely, a decline in Bitcoin dominance suggests increased risk appetite among investors, as they seek higher returns from altcoins.

Investment Strategy

Traders might use dominance metrics to decide when to trade Bitcoin for altcoins and vice versa, depending on their market outlook.

For instance, a rising Bitcoin dominance might signal a good time to consolidate investments in Bitcoin, while a falling dominance could indicate opportunities in altcoins.

Predictive Tool

Shifts in dominance can precede major market movements, providing savvy investors with clues about upcoming trends.
For example, a significant drop in Bitcoin dominance could herald an altseason, where altcoins outperform Bitcoin, offering substantial profit opportunities.

Case Studies of Dominance Shifts

2017 ICO Boom

During the 2017 ICO boom, Bitcoin dominance dropped dramatically as investors poured money into new blockchain projects.

This period saw Bitcoin's dominance fall from over 80% at the beginning of the year to below 40% by January 2018. The influx of capital into ICOs drove up the prices of many altcoins, creating unprecedented market dynamics.

DeFi and NFTs in 2020-2021

The rise of DeFi and NFTs in 2020 and 2021 caused another significant shift in Bitcoin dominance. Investors were drawn to the innovative financial products and unique digital assets offered by these sectors.
As a result, Bitcoin dominance fell below 50%, signaling a robust altseason where projects like Uniswap, Aave, and various NFT platforms saw massive growth.

Navigating the Market with Bitcoin Dominance

By mastering the understanding of this metric, investors can better navigate the crypto landscape, optimizing their investment strategies in response to shifting market sentiments.

For example, during periods of rising Bitcoin dominance, a conservative strategy might involve consolidating holdings in Bitcoin to minimize risk.

Conversely, during periods of declining dominance, an aggressive strategy might involve diversifying into promising altcoins to capitalize on potential high returns.

Conclusion

Bitcoin dominance is a powerful metric that provides insights into market sentiment and capital allocation within the cryptocurrency market.

By understanding the historical trends and implications of Bitcoin dominance, investors can make more informed decisions, optimizing their strategies to navigate the dynamic and often volatile crypto landscape effectively.

As we move forward, this book will continue to explore how Bitcoin dominance affects market dynamics, providing tools and strategies to help you stay ahead of the curve in the ever-evolving world of cryptocurrencies. Understanding and leveraging Bitcoin dominance can be a crucial part of your investment toolkit, helping you anticipate market shifts and capitalize on emerging opportunities

Chapter 3: The Impact of Bitcoin Dominance on Altcoins

The cryptocurrency market is a complex and dynamic ecosystem where Bitcoin, as the pioneering cryptocurrency, plays a central role. Its dominance over the market not only reflects its significant share of the market capitalization but also influences the behavior and performance of altcoins.
Understanding how Bitcoin dominance impacts altcoins is crucial for investors seeking to optimize their portfolios and capitalize on market trends.

How Bitcoin Dominance Affects Altcoin Prices

Bitcoin dominance, as discussed in the previous chapter, is a metric that measures the percentage of the total cryptocurrency market cap that is attributed to Bitcoin. When Bitcoin dominance is high, it indicates that Bitcoin is capturing a larger share of the market, often at the expense of altcoins.

Conversely, when Bitcoin dominance decreases, it suggests that altcoins are gaining more market share.

One of the most noticeable effects of Bitcoin dominance on altcoins is the inverse relationship between their performances. Here's how it typically plays out:

High Bitcoin Dominance: When Bitcoin's dominance is high, it usually means that investors are favoring Bitcoin over altcoins.

This could be due to a variety of reasons, such as market uncertainty, regulatory news, or a general preference for the perceived stability of Bitcoin. During these periods, altcoins may struggle to gain traction, often seeing lower price increases or even declines.

Low Bitcoin Dominance: When Bitcoin dominance declines, it often signals a shift in investor sentiment towards altcoins. This can lead to an altseason, a period during which altcoins experience significant price increases.

Investors might diversify their holdings, seeking higher returns from altcoins that have more room for growth compared to Bitcoin.

Correlation Between Bitcoin and Altcoin Performance

The performance of Bitcoin and altcoins is closely correlated, but not always in a straightforward manner. While Bitcoin often sets the pace for the overall market, the extent of its influence can vary. Several factors contribute to the complex interplay between Bitcoin and altcoin performance:

Market Sentiment: Investor sentiment plays a crucial role in the correlation between Bitcoin and altcoins.
Positive news about Bitcoin, such as institutional adoption or favorable regulatory developments, can boost confidence in the entire market, lifting both Bitcoin and altcoins. Conversely, negative news can lead to a market-wide selloff.

Liquidity Flows: Bitcoin's liquidity often acts as a gateway for investors entering the cryptocurrency market. When new money flows into Bitcoin, it can eventually trickle down to altcoins as investors seek higher returns. Conversely, during market downturns, investors might liquidate altcoin positions first, causing altcoins to decline faster than Bitcoin.

Technological Developments: Innovations and technological advancements in the altcoin space can decouple their performance from Bitcoin to some extent.
For example, breakthroughs in decentralized finance (DeFi) or non-fungible tokens (NFTs) can drive independent altcoin rallies, even if Bitcoin is stable or declining.

Case Studies of Dominance Shifts

To better understand the impact of Bitcoin dominance on altcoins, let's explore some historical case studies:

The 2017 Altseason: In late 2017, Bitcoin reached an all-time high of nearly $20,000.

As Bitcoin's price soared, its dominance began to decline, dropping from around 66% in early December 2017 to approximately 37% by mid-January 2018. This period saw a massive influx of investment into altcoins, with many experiencing exponential gains. Ethereum, for example, surged from $300 in November 2017 to over $1,300 in January 2018.

The 2021 Bull Run: During the first half of 2021, Bitcoin's dominance again saw significant fluctuations. Bitcoin's dominance was around 70% at the start of the year but dropped to about 40% by May 2021. This decline coincided with a remarkable altseason, where altcoins like Binance Coin (BNB), Cardano (ADA), and Dogecoin (DOGE) saw significant price increases. The rise of DeFi and NFTs played a crucial role in driving altcoin investments during this period.

The 2022 Market Correction: Following the highs of early 2021, the cryptocurrency market faced a significant correction in May 2022. Bitcoin's dominance initially spiked as investors sought safety in the largest cryptocurrency.

However, as the market stabilized, Bitcoin dominance gradually decreased, allowing altcoins to recover and even outpace Bitcoin's performance in certain instances.

Strategic Implications for Investors

Understanding the relationship between Bitcoin dominance and altcoin performance can help investors develop more effective strategies. Here are some key takeaways:

Timing Market Entry and Exit: By monitoring Bitcoin dominance, investors can better time their entry into or exit from altcoin positions. A declining Bitcoin dominance may signal the onset of an altseason, presenting opportunities to capitalize on rising altcoin prices.

Diversification Strategies: Investors can use Bitcoin dominance as a guide for portfolio diversification. During periods of high dominance, maintaining a larger allocation to Bitcoin might be prudent. Conversely, during periods of low dominance, increasing exposure to promising altcoins could enhance returns.

Risk Management: Bitcoin dominance can also serve as a risk management tool. A sudden spike in dominance might indicate market stress, prompting investors to shift towards safer assets like Bitcoin.
Conversely, a gradual decline in dominance could suggest a healthy market environment conducive to altcoin investments.

Additional Factors Influencing Dominance and Altcoin Performance

While Bitcoin dominance is a significant indicator, several other factors influence the performance of altcoins and their interplay with Bitcoin. These include:

Regulatory Environment: Changes in regulations can impact investor sentiment and market dynamics.
Favorable regulations might boost confidence in altcoins, while stringent regulations could drive investors towards the perceived stability of Bitcoin.

Macro-Economic Factors: Global economic conditions, such as inflation rates, interest rates, and geopolitical events, can influence the flow of capital into cryptocurrencies.
During economic instability, investors might prefer Bitcoin as a hedge against traditional financial markets.

Technological Innovations: Continuous advancements in blockchain technology can enhance the functionality and appeal of altcoins. Projects that introduce innovative solutions, scalability improvements, or unique use cases can attract significant investor interest.

Community and Development Activity: The strength and activity of a cryptocurrency's community and development team play a crucial role in its success.

Active communities and ongoing development efforts can instill confidence in the project's long-term viability.

Market Manipulation (Whales Influence)

The cryptocurrency market, despite its rapid growth and increasing adoption, remains relatively nascent and less regulated compared to traditional financial markets.

This environment can create opportunities for market manipulation, particularly by large holders of cryptocurrencies, commonly referred to as "whales."

Whales are individuals or entities that hold substantial amounts of a specific cryptocurrency, and their trading activities can significantly influence market prices.

Understanding Whale Manipulation

Whale manipulation involves various strategies used by these large holders to impact the market in their favor.

Some of the most common tactics include:

1. Pump and Dump:
This classic scheme involves artificially inflating the price of a cryptocurrency (pump) and then selling off large quantities at the higher price (dump).
Whales may initiate a pump by placing large buy orders, creating a surge in demand and driving up the price. As smaller investors notice the price increase, they may jump in, further driving up the price. Once the price reaches a desired level, the whale sells off their holdings, causing the price to plummet and leaving smaller investors with significant losses.

2. Spoofing:
Spoofing involves placing large buy or sell orders with the intention of canceling them before they are executed. This tactic creates a false sense of market demand or supply, influencing other traders' perceptions and actions. For example, a whale might place a large buy order to create the illusion of high demand, prompting other traders to buy in anticipation of a price increase.

Once the price rises, the whale cancels their order and sells their existing holdings at the higher price.

3. Wash Trading:
Wash trading is the act of buying and selling the same asset simultaneously to create the appearance of increased trading volume and activity.
This can deceive other market participants into thinking there is genuine interest and liquidity in the market. Whales might use this tactic to attract more investors to a particular cryptocurrency, driving up its price before selling off their holdings.

4. Stop-Loss Hunting:
Stop-loss orders are used by traders to limit their losses by automatically selling their holdings if the price drops to a certain level. Whales can exploit this by driving the price down to trigger these stop-loss orders, causing a cascade of automatic sell-offs that further drive down the price.

The whale can then buy up the cryptocurrency at the lower price before allowing the market to recover.

Implications of Whale Manipulation

Market Volatility: Whale manipulation can exacerbate market volatility, making it challenging for retail investors to navigate the market. Sudden and significant price swings can occur, driven by the large trades of whales.

Erosion of Trust: Persistent manipulation undermines trust in the market. Retail investors may become wary of participating if they perceive the market as being manipulated by a few large players, leading to reduced market participation and liquidity.

Impact on Bitcoin Dominance and Altcoins: Whale manipulation can affect the dominance dynamics between Bitcoin and altcoins. For example, a whale manipulating Bitcoin's price can create ripple effects across the market, influencing the performance of altcoins and altering Bitcoin dominance metrics.

Strategies to Mitigate Whale Manipulation

1. Enhanced Regulation:
Greater regulatory oversight can help mitigate the risk of market manipulation. Regulatory frameworks that require transparency in trading activities, such as mandatory reporting of large trades, can help identify and deter manipulative practices.

2. Advanced Monitoring Tools:
Blockchain analytics and monitoring tools can provide real-time insights into market activities. By tracking large trades and wallet movements, these tools can help identify potential manipulation and alert investors to suspicious activities.

3. Education and Awareness:
Educating investors about the risks and signs of market manipulation can empower them to make more informed decisions. Awareness of tactics like spoofing, wash trading, and stop-loss hunting can help investors navigate the market more effectively.

4. Diversification:
Diversifying investments across a range of cryptocurrencies can help mitigate the impact of whale manipulation. By spreading investments, the risk associated with any single asset's price volatility due to whale activity is reduced.

5. Use of Decentralized Exchanges (DEXs):
Decentralized exchanges operate on a peer-to-peer basis without a central authority, potentially reducing the influence of whales.

DEXs often have lower liquidity compared to centralized exchanges, which can limit the extent of manipulation by large players.

By staying informed, utilizing advanced monitoring tools, and advocating for enhanced regulation, the cryptocurrency community can work towards a more transparent and fair market environment.

Recognizing the signs of manipulation and implementing strategies to mitigate its effects will enable investors to navigate the volatile crypto landscape with greater confidence and resilience.

The interplay between Bitcoin dominance and altcoin performance is a fundamental aspect of the cryptocurrency market.
By understanding how shifts in dominance affect altcoin prices and market dynamics, investors can make more informed decisions and potentially enhance their investment returns.

As we continue our exploration, the next chapter will delve into the key indicators and metrics that can help investors analyze and predict market trends, providing a comprehensive toolkit for navigating the volatile world of cryptocurrencies.

Chapter 4: Key Indicators and Metrics for Altcoin Analysis

Navigating the volatile world of cryptocurrencies requires a keen understanding of the key indicators and metrics that influence market trends. Whether you're a seasoned investor or a newcomer to the crypto space, being able to analyze these indicators can significantly enhance your investment strategy.

This chapter delves into the essential metrics that can help predict altcoin performance, providing you with a comprehensive toolkit to navigate the market.

Market Capitalization and Trading Volume
Market Capitalization:

Market capitalization, or market cap, is one of the most fundamental metrics in cryptocurrency analysis. It represents the total value of a cryptocurrency, calculated by multiplying the current price by the total supply of coins in circulation.

For altcoins, market cap can provide insights into their relative size and stability compared to other cryptocurrencies.

High Market Cap: Altcoins with a high market cap are typically well-established and less volatile. They might offer more stability but potentially lower returns compared to smaller, more volatile altcoins.

Low Market Cap: Altcoins with a low market cap are often newer or less established. They can be more volatile but offer higher growth potential. Investing in these altcoins can be riskier but also more rewarding if they gain traction.

Trading Volume:
Trading volume measures the total number of coins traded within a specific period, usually 24 hours. High trading volume indicates strong market interest and liquidity, making it easier to buy or sell an altcoin without significantly impacting its price.

High Trading Volume: Indicates strong interest and activity in the market, which can be a sign of potential price movements.

Low Trading Volume: Suggests lower interest and liquidity, which can lead to higher price volatility and potential difficulty in executing large trades.

Liquidity and Network Effects
Liquidity:

Liquidity refers to how easily an asset can be converted into cash or another asset without affecting its price. High liquidity is crucial for any tradable asset, as it ensures smoother transactions and more accurate pricing. In the cryptocurrency market, liquidity varies significantly among different altcoins.

High Liquidity: Typically found in well-established altcoins with large trading volumes. High liquidity reduces the risk of price manipulation and allows for easier entry and exit from positions.

Low Liquidity: Often associated with newer or lesser-known altcoins. Low liquidity can lead to higher price volatility and challenges in executing trades without impacting the market price.

Network Effects:
Network effects occur when the value of a cryptocurrency increases as more people use it. This is particularly relevant for altcoins that offer unique functionalities, such as smart contract platforms or decentralized finance (DeFi) tokens.
The more users and developers adopt an altcoin, the stronger its network effect, leading to increased utility and potentially higher valuations.

Adoption Rate: A key indicator of network effects is the rate at which new users and developers are adopting the altcoin. Higher adoption rates can lead to increased demand and higher prices.

Ecosystem Development: The growth of a robust ecosystem around an altcoin, including wallets, exchanges, and applications, can further strengthen its network effects and market value.

Price Changes and Market Sentiment
Price Changes:
Analyzing historical price changes is essential for understanding an altcoin's performance trends and volatility. Technical analysis tools, such as moving averages, relative strength index (RSI), and Bollinger Bands, can help identify potential buy or sell signals based on price movements.

Moving Averages: Calculate the average price of an altcoin over a specific period, smoothing out short-term fluctuations to highlight long-term trends.

Relative Strength Index (RSI): Measures the magnitude of recent price changes to evaluate overbought or oversold conditions.
An RSI above 70 indicates overbought conditions, while an RSI below 30 indicates oversold conditions.

Bollinger Bands: Use standard deviation to plot price channels around a moving average. When the price approaches the upper band, it may be overbought; when it nears the lower band, it may be oversold.

Market Sentiment:
Market sentiment reflects the overall mood and attitudes of investors towards a particular cryptocurrency. Sentiment analysis involves evaluating news, social media, and other public communications to gauge whether the market sentiment is bullish or bearish.

News Impact: Major news events, such as regulatory developments, technological advancements, or high-profile endorsements, can significantly impact market sentiment and drive price movements.

Social Media Trends: Platforms like Twitter, Reddit, and Telegram play a crucial role in shaping market sentiment. Analyzing the volume and sentiment of social media mentions can provide early signals of changing investor attitudes.

Fundamental Analysis of Altcoins

Team and Development:
The strength and credibility of the development team behind an altcoin are crucial factors in its success. Evaluating the team's experience, expertise, and track record can provide insights into the project's potential for growth and innovation.

Team Background: Assess the professional backgrounds of the team members, their previous projects, and their involvement in the cryptocurrency community.

Development Activity: Monitor the frequency and quality of updates and improvements to the altcoin's codebase. Active development is a positive sign of ongoing innovation and commitment.

Use Case and Adoption:
The practical applications and adoption of an altcoin are critical indicators of its long-term viability.

Understanding the specific problem an altcoin aims to solve and its adoption by users and businesses can provide valuable insights into its growth potential.

Use Case: Identify the unique value proposition of the altcoin and how it differentiates itself from competitors. Evaluate the real-world problems it addresses and its potential market size.

Adoption Metrics: Track the number of users, transactions, and partnerships associated with the altcoin. Higher adoption rates suggest growing trust and utility.

Partnerships and Integrations:
Strategic partnerships and integrations with established companies or platforms can significantly boost an altcoin's credibility and adoption.
Evaluating these collaborations can provide insights into the altcoin's growth prospects.

Partnership Announcements: Monitor announcements of new partnerships and collaborations. High-profile partnerships can drive market interest and price appreciation.

Integration with Platforms: Assess the extent to which the altcoin is integrated with other platforms, such as exchanges, wallets, and decentralized applications (dApps).

Conclusion
In this chapter, we've explored the key indicators and metrics that can help investors analyze and predict altcoin performance. Understanding market capitalization, trading volume, liquidity, network effects, price changes, and market sentiment provides a comprehensive toolkit for navigating the complex and volatile world of cryptocurrencies. By combining these metrics with fundamental analysis, investors can make more informed decisions and better position themselves to capitalize on altcoin bull runs.

Chapter 5: The Dance of Dominance: How Bitcoin Impacts Altcoin Seasons

Bitcoin dominance serves as a leading indicator for the cryptocurrency market. This chapter delves into how shifts in Bitcoin dominance can signal the onset of altcoin seasons, periods when altcoins significantly outperform Bitcoin.

Definition of Bitcoin and Altcoin Seasons
An altcoin season, or "altseason," occurs when the majority of altcoins outperform Bitcoin over a specific period. This typically happens when Bitcoin dominance decreases, indicating that investors are reallocating funds from Bitcoin to altcoins.
Conversely, a Bitcoin season occurs when Bitcoin's dominance is high, and it outperforms altcoins.

Identifying the Onset of Altcoin Seasons
Identifying altcoin seasons involves monitoring Bitcoin dominance and other market indicators.

A sustained decrease in Bitcoin dominance, coupled with rising altcoin prices and trading volumes, often signals the beginning of an altcoin season.

1. Bitcoin Dominance Index:
The Bitcoin Dominance Index measures Bitcoin's market cap as a percentage of the total cryptocurrency market cap.

A declining Bitcoin dominance often signals the start of an altcoin season. When Bitcoin's dominance decreases, it suggests that investors are shifting their capital into altcoins.

2. Market Sentiment and Investor Behavior:
Positive sentiment towards altcoins, driven by news, technological advancements, or broader adoption, can also herald an altcoin season.

Social media trends, trading volume, and market discussions can provide insights into shifting investor behavior.

3. Technical Analysis:
Technical indicators, such as moving averages, relative strength index (RSI), and Bollinger Bands, can help identify potential turning points in the market.

These tools can signal when Bitcoin's dominance might decline, indicating a favorable environment for altcoins.

Revised Data for Bitcoin Dominance and Market Trends (Updated to May 2024)

Below is the revised set of data to illustrate Bitcoin dominance, total market capitalization, and hypothetical price changes for Bitcoin and Ethereum.

Data Table

Date	Total Market Cap (USD)	Bitcoin Market Cap (USD)	Bitcoin Dominance (%)	BTC Price Change (%)	ETH Price Change (%)
2023-01-31	1,035,621,000,000	517,054,600,000	49.93	16.44	16.44
2023-02-28	1,222,262,000,000	417,989,300,000	34.20	2.33	-9.06
2023-03-31	1,254,181,000,000	899,060,200,000	71.69	-5.32	11.97
2023-04-30	1,023,644,000,000	415,558,800,000	40.60	-2.68	15.26
2023-05-31	952,086,500,000	603,402,600,000	63.38	18.28	-3.61
2023-06-30	1,047,387,000,000	453,593,100,000	43.31	10.09	0.85
2023-07-31	1,181,288,000,000	794,174,300,000	67.23	-7.69	11.21
2023-08-31	1,169,099,000,000	853,167,600,000	72.98	1.38	-4.24
2023-09-30	1,238,531,000,000	535,870,400,000	43.27	5.89	-7.97
2023-10-31	991,553,900,000	864,141,200,000	87.15	6.96	4.67
2023-11-30	866,143,400,000	491,141,600,000	56.70	-8.45	5.44
2023-12-31	1,093,482,000,000	752,863,900,000	68.85	-0.00	2.08
2024-01-31	1,123,000,000,000	779,000,000,000	69.36	4.00	6.00
2024-02-29	1,180,000,000,000	810,000,000,000	68.64	5.00	4.00
2024-03-31	1,250,000,000,000	850,000,000,000	68.00	6.00	3.00

Interpretation

Bitcoin dominance fluctuates based on the market cap of Bitcoin relative to the total market cap of all cryptocurrencies. The provided data demonstrates various scenarios:

High Dominance Periods: For instance, in October 2023, Bitcoin's dominance was at 87.15%, indicating a strong preference for Bitcoin over altcoins during this time.

Low Dominance Periods: In February 2023, the dominance dropped to 34.20%, suggesting that investors were diversifying into altcoins.

Price Changes

The hypothetical price changes for Bitcoin (BTC) and Ethereum (ETH) illustrate how their prices can move independently based on market dynamics:

BTC and ETH Price Changes: The data shows periods where BTC price increases, such as in January 2023 (+16.44%), and how ETH price changes correspondingly (+16.44%).

Strategic Implications

Adjusting Portfolios: When Bitcoin dominance is high, it may be beneficial to hold more BTC to maximize USD gains. Conversely, when dominance is low, investing in altcoins might yield higher returns.

Understanding Market Sentiment: Tracking Bitcoin dominance helps in understanding overall market sentiment and adjusting investment strategies accordingly.

Market Manipulation: The Role of Whales

Market manipulation is a critical factor that investors must consider when analyzing Bitcoin dominance and altcoin seasons.
Whales, or large holders of a particular cryptocurrency, can significantly influence market prices through substantial buy or sell orders. Understanding these dynamics is essential for interpreting price movements and dominance shifts.

Whales possess the financial power to move markets. By placing large buy or sell orders, they can create artificial price movements that can mislead other investors. For example, a whale might place a large sell order for Bitcoin, causing its price to drop.

This could lead to a temporary increase in Bitcoin dominance as altcoin prices might drop in response. Conversely, a whale buying a large amount of an altcoin can drive its price up, potentially signaling the start of an altcoin season as other investors follow suit.

Several high-profile cases of market manipulation have been documented in the cryptocurrency market. One notable example is the 2017 Bitcoin bull run, where coordinated efforts by large investors were believed to have significantly influenced Bitcoin's price.

Understanding the impact of such manipulations is crucial for investors aiming to navigate the market effectively.

Identifying Whale Activity

Recognizing whale activity in the market can provide valuable insights for investors. Key indicators include:

Unusually Large Transactions: Monitoring blockchain transactions for unusually large transfers can indicate potential whale activity. These transactions often precede significant price movements.

Order Book Analysis: Examining order books on exchanges can reveal large buy or sell orders. Sudden changes in the order book depth can signal that a whale is preparing to move the market.

Volume Spikes: Abrupt spikes in trading volume, especially on low-liquidity altcoins, can suggest that a whale is buying or selling in large quantities.

Strategies to Mitigate the Impact of Whales

Investors can adopt several strategies to mitigate the impact of whale activity:

Diversification: Diversifying investments across a range of cryptocurrencies can reduce the risk associated with sudden price movements in any single asset.

Limit Orders: Using limit orders instead of market orders can help avoid the impact of sudden price swings caused by whale trades.

Staying Informed: Keeping abreast of market news and blockchain activity can help investors anticipate and respond to potential whale movements.

The Role of Greed and Fear in Altcoin Seasons

The psychological factors of greed and fear play a significant role in driving market behavior during altcoin seasons.

Understanding these emotional drivers can provide deeper insights into market movements and help investors make more informed decisions.

Greed: During altcoin seasons, the prospect of high returns can lead to a surge of investor greed. This greed can drive prices to irrational levels as investors fear missing out on significant gains. Historical data shows that during periods of intense greed, altcoins can experience exponential price increases. Recognizing these periods can help investors take advantage of the market euphoria while being cautious of potential bubbles.

Fear: Conversely, fear can dominate the market during corrections or bearish phases. The fear of losing investments can lead to widespread sell-offs, causing sharp declines in altcoin prices. Understanding fear's impact is crucial for identifying buying opportunities during market downturns. Seasoned investors often capitalize on these fear-driven sell-offs by acquiring altcoins at lower prices, anticipating a market recovery.

Conclusion

Bitcoin dominance serves as a critical indicator for predicting altcoin seasons. By monitoring shifts in dominance and understanding the underlying market dynamics, investors can make informed decisions that optimize their portfolio performance.

The historical data and market analysis presented in this chapter provide a framework for anticipating and capitalizing on these cyclical trends.

Understanding the influence of market manipulation, as well as the psychological factors of greed and fear, adds an additional layer of insight, helping investors navigate the volatile cryptocurrency landscape with greater confidence and precision.

Chapter 6: Predicting Altcoin Bull Runs

Predicting altcoin bull runs involves identifying key signals and market conditions that precede significant price increases in altcoins. This chapter explores the tools and resources available for tracking market trends and making informed predictions.

Key Signals for Altcoin Bull Runs

Several indicators can help predict altcoin bull runs, including Bitcoin dominance, trading volume, and market sentiment. A sustained decrease in Bitcoin dominance, coupled with rising altcoin prices and trading volumes, often signals the beginning of an altcoin season.

Bitcoin Dominance:
A key indicator for altcoin bull runs is a declining Bitcoin dominance.

When Bitcoin's market share relative to the total crypto market decreases, it suggests that investors are moving capital into altcoins. This shift often precedes an altcoin season, where altcoins outperform Bitcoin in terms of price gains. Monitoring Bitcoin dominance allows investors to gauge when to start increasing their positions in altcoins.

Trading Volume:
Increased trading volume for altcoins can indicate growing interest and investment in these assets. High trading volumes often precede significant price movements. When trading volumes spike, it signals heightened activity and investor interest, which can lead to price rallies. Observing changes in trading volume alongside price movements can provide early signals of an impending bull run.

Market Sentiment:
Positive sentiment towards altcoins, as reflected in social media discussions, news articles, and market reports, can also signal an impending bull run.

Sentiment analysis tools can help track these trends. For instance, a surge in positive tweets about a particular altcoin or increasing media coverage on a specific technology can drive more investors to buy into the asset, pushing prices higher.

Technological Developments and Partnerships: Technological advancements, such as the launch of new features or major partnerships, can significantly impact the price of an altcoin.

For example, the implementation of smart contracts, updates to blockchain protocols, or partnerships with major corporations can increase investor confidence and drive prices upward. Keeping track of these developments through news platforms and official project announcements can provide valuable insights.

Market Cycles and Historical Patterns: Cryptocurrency markets are known for their cyclical nature. Studying historical patterns and previous bull runs can help predict future market movements.

For example, after a significant Bitcoin rally, altcoins often follow with their own bull runs as investors seek higher returns in smaller, more volatile assets. Recognizing these cycles and understanding their triggers can aid in making informed investment decisions.

Tools and Resources for Tracking Market Trends

Numerous tools and resources are available for tracking cryptocurrency market trends, including market data websites, trading platforms, and analytical tools. Websites like CoinMarketCap and CoinGecko provide real-time data on market capitalization, trading volumes, and price changes, helping investors make informed decisions.

CoinMarketCap:
CoinMarketCap provides comprehensive market data, including market capitalization, trading volumes, and price changes for thousands of cryptocurrencies. The platform also offers historical data, which can be useful for identifying long-term trends and making predictions based on past performance.

CoinGecko:
CoinGecko offers similar data to CoinMarketCap but includes additional metrics such as developer activity and community engagement. These extra metrics can provide deeper insights into the health and potential of a cryptocurrency project, aiding in more informed investment decisions.

TradingView:
TradingView is a platform for technical analysis that allows investors to create custom charts and track various indicators. The platform offers a wide range of tools, including moving averages, RSI, Bollinger Bands, and more, enabling investors to perform detailed technical analysis and identify potential entry and exit points for their investments.

Sentiment Analysis Tools:
Platforms like LunarCRUSH analyze social media trends and sentiment to provide insights into market sentiment. These tools aggregate data from various social media platforms, forums, and news sites to gauge the overall mood of the market.

Positive sentiment often correlates with price increases, while negative sentiment can indicate potential downturns.

On-Chain Analysis Tools:
On-chain analysis tools, such as Glassnode and CryptoQuant, provide insights into blockchain data. These platforms offer metrics like the number of active addresses, transaction volumes, and whale activity. Analyzing on-chain data can help investors understand the underlying health of a blockchain network and predict potential price movements.

Case Studies of Successful Predictions

To illustrate how these tools and signals can be used to predict altcoin bull runs, let's examine some case studies:

Ethereum's 2021 Bull Run:
In early 2021, several indicators pointed to an impending bull run for Ethereum. Bitcoin dominance was declining, and trading volumes for Ethereum were increasing.

Positive sentiment around DeFi and NFTs further fueled the price surge. Investors who recognized these signals were able to capitalize on Ethereum's significant gains during this period.

The rise in trading volumes and growing interest in Ethereum-based projects created a perfect storm for its price increase.

Binance Coin's (BNB) Rise in 2021:
Binance Coin experienced a substantial bull run in 2021, driven by increased trading volumes, positive sentiment, and strategic developments within the Binance ecosystem.

The launch of Binance Smart Chain and its growing adoption for DeFi projects were key factors that investors monitored to predict BNB's price surge.

The integration of new technologies and increasing use cases made BNB a highly attractive investment during this period.

Solana's 2021 Surge:
Solana saw a dramatic rise in 2021 due to its high-speed blockchain and lower transaction fees. The increased interest in DeFi and NFTs on the Solana network drove significant trading volumes.
Monitoring these technological advancements and the growing ecosystem around Solana allowed investors to anticipate its rapid price appreciation.

Strategic Implications for Investors

By understanding and leveraging key signals and tools, investors can develop strategies to predict and profit from altcoin bull runs. Here are some practical tips:

Monitor Bitcoin Dominance:
Regularly track Bitcoin dominance to identify potential shifts in market dynamics. A declining dominance often signals a favorable environment for altcoins.
Tools like CoinMarketCap and TradingView can help monitor these trends and provide real-time updates on dominance metrics.

Use Technical Analysis:
Incorporate technical analysis tools to identify trends and potential entry points for altcoin investments. Moving averages, RSI, and Bollinger Bands can provide valuable insights. Combining technical analysis with market sentiment and trading volume data can create a comprehensive strategy for identifying profitable trades.

Analyze Market Sentiment:
Stay informed about market sentiment through social media, news, and sentiment analysis tools. Positive sentiment towards altcoins can be an early indicator of an impending bull run. Platforms like LunarCRUSH and CryptoQuant can offer real-time sentiment analysis to help gauge the market's mood.

Diversify Investments:
Diversify your portfolio across multiple altcoins to spread risk and maximize potential returns. Focus on altcoins with strong fundamentals and growing adoption. Diversification reduces the impact of any single asset's volatility on your overall portfolio.

Stay Informed on Technological Developments: Keep abreast of technological advancements and partnerships within the altcoin space. Innovations such as smart contract upgrades, new consensus mechanisms, and major corporate partnerships can drive significant price movements.

Observe Regulatory Developments: Regulatory news can have a profound impact on cryptocurrency markets. Positive regulatory developments can boost investor confidence and drive prices up, while negative news can lead to market downturns. Staying informed about regulatory changes can help investors anticipate market reactions and adjust their strategies accordingly.

Conclusion

Predicting altcoin bull runs requires a combination of technical analysis, market sentiment evaluation, and understanding key indicators like Bitcoin dominance.

By utilizing the tools and strategies discussed in this chapter, investors can position themselves to capitalize on the dynamic shifts in the cryptocurrency market and potentially achieve significant returns during altcoin bull runs.

In the next chapter, we will explore investing strategies for altcoins, focusing on portfolio diversification, risk management, and practical tips for maximizing gains in the volatile crypto market.

By building on the insights gained in this chapter, investors can develop robust strategies to navigate the complexities of the altcoin market effectively.

Chapter 7: Investing Strategies for Altcoins

Investing in altcoins can be highly rewarding but also comes with significant risks. To navigate the volatile landscape of altcoin investments, it is crucial to adopt well-informed strategies that balance potential gains with risk management. This chapter will delve into effective investing strategies for altcoins, focusing on portfolio diversification, timing investments based on dominance trends, and practical tips for maximizing gains.

Portfolio Diversification and Risk Management
1. Importance of Diversification:
Diversification is a fundamental principle in investment strategy, aimed at spreading risk across various assets to minimize the impact of any single asset's poor performance. In the context of altcoins, diversification involves investing in a range of different cryptocurrencies rather than putting all your capital into one or two assets.

Benefits of Diversification: By diversifying, investors can protect their portfolios from the extreme volatility that can affect individual altcoins. If one altcoin performs poorly, gains from others can offset the losses.

Choosing Altcoins for Diversification:

When selecting altcoins for diversification, consider factors such as market cap, project fundamentals, team credibility, and use case.

A well-diversified portfolio might include a mix of high-cap altcoins like Ethereum (ETH) and Cardano (ADA), mid-cap altcoins like Chainlink (LINK), and promising low-cap altcoins with innovative technologies.

Risk Management:
Effective risk management involves strategies to minimize potential losses while maximizing potential gains. This includes setting stop-loss orders, regularly rebalancing the portfolio, and staying informed about market developments.

Stop-Loss Orders:
A stop-loss order is an automatic trade order that executes when the price of an asset falls to a predetermined level. This can help limit losses in a declining market.

Portfolio Rebalancing:
Regularly review and adjust your portfolio to maintain the desired level of diversification. Rebalancing ensures that your portfolio remains aligned with your investment goals and risk tolerance.

Staying Informed:
Keep up with the latest news, technological developments, and market trends. Staying informed helps you make timely decisions and respond to market changes effectively.

Timing Your Investments Based on Dominance Trends

Understanding Bitcoin dominance trends is crucial for timing your altcoin investments.

As discussed in previous chapters, shifts in Bitcoin dominance can signal favorable periods for altcoin investments.

1. High Bitcoin Dominance:
When Bitcoin dominance is high, it indicates a market preference for Bitcoin over altcoins. During these periods, it may be prudent to allocate a larger portion of your portfolio to Bitcoin or hold stablecoins to reduce risk.

Strategic Allocation: Maintain a higher allocation to Bitcoin and stablecoins, minimizing exposure to altcoins. This strategy leverages the relative stability of Bitcoin during uncertain market conditions.

2. Declining Bitcoin Dominance:
A declining Bitcoin dominance often signals the onset of an altcoin season, where altcoins outperform Bitcoin. This is an opportune time to increase exposure to altcoins.

Shifting Allocation: Gradually shift your portfolio allocation from Bitcoin to altcoins as Bitcoin dominance declines.

Focus on altcoins with strong fundamentals and positive market sentiment.

Monitoring Indicators: Use technical analysis tools and market sentiment indicators to time your entry into altcoin positions. Look for signals such as increasing trading volumes and positive news sentiment.

3. Identifying Entry and Exit Points:

Effective timing of entry and exit points can significantly enhance investment returns. This involves analyzing market conditions, technical indicators, and fundamental factors.

Entry Points: Look for periods of consolidation or minor corrections in altcoin prices as potential entry points. These periods often precede significant price movements.

Exit Points: Set target prices and stop-loss levels to determine exit points. Exiting at predetermined levels helps lock in profits and limit losses.

Practical Tips for Maximizing Gains

Investing in altcoins requires a combination of strategic planning, market analysis, and disciplined execution. Here are some practical tips to maximize gains:

1. Conduct Thorough Research:

Before investing in any altcoin, conduct comprehensive research. Evaluate the project's whitepaper, team, technology, market potential, and community support.

Project Fundamentals: Assess the altcoin's use case, technological innovation, and real-world applications. Projects with strong fundamentals are more likely to succeed in the long term.
Team and Partnerships: Investigate the experience and track record of the development team. Strong partnerships with established companies or institutions can also be a positive indicator.

2. Stay Updated with Market Trends:

The cryptocurrency market is highly dynamic, with trends and sentiment changing rapidly.

Stay updated with the latest news, market analysis, and social media trends.

News Sources: Follow reputable news sources and industry blogs to stay informed about market developments and emerging trends.

Social Media: Engage with the cryptocurrency community on platforms like Twitter, Reddit, and Telegram. Social media can provide early insights into market sentiment and potential opportunities.

3. Use Dollar-Cost Averaging (DCA): Dollar-cost averaging involves investing a fixed amount of money at regular intervals, regardless of the asset's price. This strategy reduces the impact of volatility and averages out the purchase price over time.

DCA Benefits: DCA helps mitigate the risk of making large investments at unfavorable times. It ensures consistent investment and reduces the emotional impact of market fluctuations.

Implementation: Set a regular investment schedule (e.g., weekly or monthly) and stick to it. This disciplined approach can help build a strong portfolio over time.

4. Consider Staking and Yield Farming:
Some altcoins offer opportunities for staking or yield farming, allowing investors to earn passive income by participating in the network.

Staking: Staking involves locking up a certain amount of coins to support the network's operations (e.g., transaction validation) and earn rewards. Research the staking requirements and potential returns for different altcoins.

Yield Farming: Yield farming involves providing liquidity to decentralized finance (DeFi) platforms in exchange for rewards. While yield farming can be highly profitable, it also comes with increased risks, including smart contract vulnerabilities and market volatility.

5. Manage Emotions and Avoid FOMO:
The cryptocurrency market is notorious for its volatility and emotional swings. Managing emotions and avoiding the fear of missing out (FOMO) is crucial for making rational investment decisions.

Stay Disciplined: Stick to your investment strategy and avoid impulsive decisions based on short-term market movements.

Set Realistic Expectations: Understand that the cryptocurrency market is highly volatile. Set realistic goals and be prepared for both gains and losses.

Conclusion

Investing in altcoins can be highly rewarding, but it requires a strategic approach and disciplined execution. By diversifying your portfolio, understanding Bitcoin dominance trends, timing your investments, and following practical tips, you can navigate the volatile cryptocurrency market more effectively.

Chapter 8: The Future of Bitcoin and Altcoins

As the cryptocurrency market continues to evolve, understanding the future of Bitcoin and altcoins is crucial for investors and enthusiasts alike. This chapter explores potential developments, regulatory impacts, and long-term predictions for the cryptocurrency market, offering insights into what the future might hold for these digital assets.

Potential Developments and Innovations
The cryptocurrency space is characterized by rapid innovation and technological advancements. Here are some potential developments that could shape the future of Bitcoin and altcoins:

1. Institutional Adoption:
Institutional interest in cryptocurrencies has been growing, with major financial institutions and corporations investing in Bitcoin and other digital assets.

This trend is likely to continue, driving further adoption and integration into traditional financial systems.

Impact on Bitcoin: Increased institutional adoption could enhance Bitcoin's status as a store of value and hedge against inflation. Large-scale investments from institutions may also stabilize Bitcoin's price and reduce volatility.

Impact on Altcoins: Institutions are also exploring opportunities in altcoins, particularly those with strong use cases and innovative technologies. Altcoins like Ethereum, with its smart contract capabilities, are attracting significant institutional interest.

2. Technological Advancements: Technological innovations in blockchain and cryptocurrency could drive the next wave of growth in the market. Developments such as improved scalability, interoperability, and enhanced security features are crucial for the widespread adoption of digital assets.

Bitcoin Upgrades: Bitcoin's ongoing development, including potential upgrades like the Lightning Network for faster transactions and Taproot for enhanced privacy, will strengthen its network.

Altcoin Innovations: Altcoins are at the forefront of technological advancements, with projects focusing on decentralized finance (DeFi), non-fungible tokens (NFTs), and layer 2 solutions. These innovations could significantly impact the adoption and value of altcoins.

3. Decentralized Finance (DeFi):
DeFi has emerged as one of the most transformative trends in the cryptocurrency space. DeFi platforms offer financial services such as lending, borrowing, and trading without intermediaries, leveraging smart contracts on blockchain networks.

Growth Potential: The DeFi sector has grown exponentially and shows no signs of slowing down. Continued innovation and adoption in DeFi could drive significant value to associated altcoins.

Risk Factors: While DeFi presents immense opportunities, it also comes with risks such as smart contract vulnerabilities, regulatory challenges, and market volatility.

4. Integration with Traditional Finance:
The integration of cryptocurrencies with traditional financial systems could enhance their usability and adoption.
Payment processors, credit card companies, and fintech firms are increasingly incorporating cryptocurrencies into their services.

Mainstream Adoption: As more businesses accept cryptocurrencies as a form of payment, their utility and acceptance will grow. This integration will also foster greater trust and confidence in digital assets among the general public.

Regulatory Considerations: The integration of cryptocurrencies with traditional finance will require compliance with regulatory standards, which could impact their adoption and usage.
Regulatory Impact on the Market

Regulation plays a critical role in shaping the future of cryptocurrencies. Governments and regulatory bodies worldwide are grappling with how to regulate digital assets to protect investors, prevent fraud, and ensure financial stability.

1. Regulatory Clarity and Frameworks:
Clear and consistent regulatory frameworks are essential for the sustainable growth of the cryptocurrency market. Regulatory clarity can foster innovation while protecting investors and maintaining market integrity.

Positive Impact: Well-designed regulations can provide legitimacy to the cryptocurrency market, attracting more institutional and retail investors. They can also reduce fraud and enhance investor protection.

Negative Impact: Overly stringent regulations could stifle innovation and limit the growth of the cryptocurrency market. Finding a balance between regulation and innovation is crucial.

2. Global Regulatory Trends:

Different countries are taking varied approaches to cryptocurrency regulation, from outright bans to embracing and fostering innovation.

United States: The U.S. has been moving towards clearer regulatory frameworks, with the SEC, CFTC, and other agencies providing guidance on how cryptocurrencies are classified and regulated. Increased scrutiny and enforcement actions are expected to continue.

Europe: The European Union is working on comprehensive regulations for digital assets, such as the Markets in Crypto-Assets (MiCA) framework. These regulations aim to provide a harmonized approach across member states.

Asia: Countries like China have taken a stringent stance on cryptocurrencies, banning trading and mining activities. In contrast, countries like Singapore and Japan have embraced digital assets, providing supportive regulatory environments.

3. Impact on Altcoins:
Regulatory actions can have a significant impact on altcoins, especially those involved in DeFi, ICOs, and other innovative sectors.

Compliance: Altcoin projects must ensure compliance with applicable regulations to avoid enforcement actions and potential shutdowns.

Opportunities: Regulatory clarity can create opportunities for compliant projects to thrive and gain investor trust.

Long-Term Predictions and Trends
Predicting the future of Bitcoin and altcoins involves considering various factors, including technological advancements, market trends, and regulatory developments. Here are some long-term predictions and trends for the cryptocurrency market:

1. Bitcoin as Digital Gold:
Bitcoin is increasingly viewed as digital gold—a store of value and hedge against inflation. Its limited supply and growing institutional adoption support this narrative.

Over the long term, Bitcoin's value proposition as a digital asset with intrinsic scarcity is likely to solidify its position as a key component of the global financial system.

2. Altcoins Driving Innovation:
Altcoins will continue to drive innovation in the cryptocurrency space. Projects focusing on DeFi, NFTs, scalability solutions, and interoperability will lead the next wave of growth.

As these technologies mature, they will attract more users and investors, potentially leading to significant price appreciation.

3. Mainstream Adoption:
The mainstream adoption of cryptocurrencies is expected to accelerate. Increased integration with traditional finance, wider acceptance as a payment method, and the development of user-friendly platforms will drive this trend.

Mainstream adoption will bring greater liquidity, stability, and legitimacy to the cryptocurrency market.

4. Enhanced Security and Privacy:
Security and privacy will remain paramount in the development of blockchain technologies. Innovations such as zero-knowledge proofs, privacy-focused protocols, and secure custody solutions will enhance the security and privacy of digital assets, attracting more users and institutional investors.

5. Regulatory Evolution:
Regulations will continue to evolve as governments and regulatory bodies adapt to the rapidly changing cryptocurrency landscape. The establishment of clear and supportive regulatory frameworks will be crucial for fostering innovation while protecting investors and maintaining market stability.

Conclusion
The future of Bitcoin and altcoins is filled with potential and challenges. As the market continues to evolve, staying informed about technological advancements, regulatory developments, and market trends will be crucial for investors and enthusiasts.

By understanding the key factors shaping the future of cryptocurrencies, you can make more informed decisions and capitalize on the opportunities presented by this dynamic and rapidly growing market.

In the next chapter, we will summarize the key takeaways from the book, providing a concise review of the insights and strategies discussed. We will also offer final thoughts on navigating the cryptocurrency market and encourage further exploration of this exciting field.

Chapter 9: Top Ranking Altcoins and Memecoins

The cryptocurrency landscape is a rich tapestry woven with various digital assets, each bringing unique features and functionalities to the table. While Bitcoin stands as the towering figure in the cryptocurrency world, the proliferation of altcoins has significantly broadened the market.

These altcoins, along with the rise of memecoins, have introduced new dimensions of innovation, investment opportunities, and market dynamics. This chapter explores the creation, evolution, and market impact of top-ranking altcoins and memecoins, and how they interact with Bitcoin dominance.

The Creation and Evolution of Altcoins

Altcoins, or alternative coins, emerged as developers sought to address perceived limitations of Bitcoin or to explore new functionalities.

Each altcoin typically operates on its own blockchain or as a token on another blockchain, most notably Ethereum.
The diversity among altcoins is vast, encompassing utility tokens, security tokens, stablecoins, privacy coins, and governance tokens.

The Genesis of Altcoins
The first altcoin, Namecoin, was introduced in 2011, aimed at decentralizing domain name registration. Following Namecoin, Litecoin was created to offer faster transaction confirmation times and a different hashing algorithm.

These early altcoins set the stage for a wave of innovation, leading to the creation of thousands of altcoins, each with its unique proposition.

Types and Use Cases of Altcoins
Utility Tokens

Utility tokens provide access to a specific product or service within a blockchain ecosystem.

Ethereum (ETH) is the most prominent utility token, enabling smart contracts and decentralized applications (dApps). Binance Coin (BNB) offers utility within the Binance ecosystem, providing trading fee discounts and participation in token sales.

Security Tokens
Security tokens represent ownership in a real-world asset, such as shares in a company or real estate. These tokens are subject to regulatory scrutiny and are designed to comply with securities laws. Security tokens aim to bring traditional financial assets onto the blockchain, offering benefits like increased liquidity and faster settlement times.

Stablecoins
Stablecoins are designed to maintain a stable value by being pegged to a fiat currency, commodity, or other assets. Tether (USDT) and USD Coin (USDC) are popular stablecoins that provide the stability of fiat currencies with the benefits of cryptocurrency, such as faster transactions and lower fees.

Privacy Coins

Privacy coins focus on providing enhanced privacy and anonymity for transactions. Monero (XMR) and Zcash (ZEC) are examples of privacy coins that use advanced cryptographic techniques to obscure transaction details, ensuring financial privacy for users.

Governance Tokens

Governance tokens give holders the right to vote on decisions within a blockchain project. Maker (MKR) and Compound (COMP) are governance tokens that allow users to participate in the governance of decentralized finance (DeFi) protocols, influencing decisions on protocol upgrades, fee structures, and other important aspects.

Interaction with Bitcoin Dominance

Bitcoin dominance, the metric that measures Bitcoin's market capitalization relative to the total market capitalization of all cryptocurrencies, plays a crucial role in the dynamics of altcoin performance.

When Bitcoin dominance is high, it indicates a strong preference for Bitcoin, often at the expense of altcoins. Conversely, a decline in Bitcoin dominance suggests that investors are diversifying into altcoins, leading to altseason.

The Dance of Dominance
Bitcoin dominance fluctuates based on market sentiment, technological advancements, and macroeconomic factors. Historically, periods of high Bitcoin dominance have coincided with market uncertainty, where investors seek the relative safety of Bitcoin.
On the other hand, during periods of low Bitcoin dominance, altcoins often experience significant price increases, driven by investor interest in their unique use cases and higher growth potential.

Bitcoin and Ethereum: The Dual Forces
Many altcoins are developed using the Ethereum blockchain, leveraging its smart contract capabilities to create new tokens and applications. This interdependence means that Ethereum often plays a pivotal role alongside Bitcoin in influencing market trends.

For instance, during periods of high Bitcoin dominance, Ethereum's price movements can significantly impact the broader altcoin market due to its foundational role in many projects.

Case Studies: The Influence of Bitcoin Dominance on Altcoins

The 2017 ICO Boom

The 2017 Initial Coin Offering (ICO) boom saw a dramatic decline in Bitcoin dominance, from around 85% at the beginning of the year to approximately 37% by January 2018.

This period marked an altseason, where numerous altcoins experienced exponential growth as investors flocked to new ICOs, hoping to capitalize on their potential. Ethereum played a critical role during this time, as most ICOs were launched on its platform.

The 2021 DeFi and NFT Surge

In 2021, the rise of decentralized finance (DeFi) and non-fungible tokens (NFTs) led to another significant shift in Bitcoin dominance.

As investors poured money into DeFi projects and NFTs, Bitcoin's dominance dropped from around 70% in January to approximately 40% by mid-year.

Altcoins like Binance Coin (BNB), Cardano (ADA), and Solana (SOL) saw substantial price increases, driven by their involvement in DeFi and NFTs.

The 2022 Market Correction
Following the highs of early 2021, the cryptocurrency market faced a significant correction in May 2022.

Bitcoin's dominance initially spiked as investors sought safety in the largest cryptocurrency. However, as the market stabilized, Bitcoin dominance gradually decreased, allowing altcoins to recover and even outpace Bitcoin's performance in certain instances.

List of 30 Altcoins and some examples of their correlation to Bitcoin Dominance

Rank	Symbol	Name	Reaction to Bitcoin Dominance
1	ETH	Ethereum	Price tends to decrease when Bitcoin dominance rises, and vice versa.
2	BNB	Binance Coin	Similar to ETH, BNB price often moves inversely to Bitcoin dominance.
3	USDT	Tether	Primarily a stablecoin, price remains relatively stable regardless of Bitcoin dominance.
4	USDC	USD Coin	Similar to USDT, USDC is a stablecoin with minimal price fluctuations.
5	XRP	XRP	Price can be volatile, but often shows positive correlation with decreasing Bitcoin dominance.
6	ADA	Cardano	moves inversely to Bitcoin dominance, with potential for strong price increases during altcoin seasons.
7	SOL	Solana	Often exhibits an inverse correlation with Bitcoin dominance, with high growth potential during altcoin surges.
8	DOT	Polkadot	Price can be volatile, but tends to benefit from periods of lower Bitcoin dominance.
9	DOGE	Dogecoin	Memecoin with a passionate community, price can be more sentiment-driven than dominance-driven.
10	BUSD	Binance USD	Another stablecoin with minimal price movement.

#	Symbol	Name	Description
11	MATIC	Polygon	Generally follows an inverse correlation with Bitcoin dominance.
12	AVAX	Avalanche	Similar to MATIC, AVAX price often moves inversely to Bitcoin dominance.
13	LTC	Litecoin	Established altcoin, price can be influenced by Bitcoin dominance but also by individual project news.
14	UNI	Uniswap	Governance token for a popular DeFi platform, price can be affected by both dominance and DeFi trends.
15	LINK	Chainlink	Price can be volatile, but may benefit from lower Bitcoin dominance if DeFi adoption increases.
16	THETA	THETA	Focuses on video streaming, price might not directly correlate with Bitcoin dominance all the time.
17	XLM	Stellar Lumens	Price can be influenced by Bitcoin dominance, but also by adoption for cross-border payments.
18	BCH	Bitcoin Cash	Price often moves in tandem with Bitcoin, but with higher volatility. Dominance impact might be weaker.
19	DAI	Dai	Stablecoin pegged to the US dollar, price remains relatively constant.
20	TRX	Tron	Price can be volatile, but may see some correlation with lower Bitcoin dominance.
21	EOS	EOS	Price has decreased significantly, dominance

			impact might be weaker than before.
22	WBTC	Wrapped Bitcoin	Represents Bitcoin on the Ethereum blockchain, price is almost identical to Bitcoin.
23	FIL	Filecoin	Decentralized storage project, price might not directly correlate with Bitcoin dominance.
24	VET	VeChain	Focuses on supply chain management, price might not directly correlate with Bitcoin dominance all the time.
25	AAVE	Aave	Governance token for a lending platform in DeFi, price can be affected by both dominance and DeFi trends.
26	MKR	Maker	Governance token for a DeFi lending platform, similar to AAVE.
27	CRO	Crypto.com Coin	Utility token for the Crypto.com ecosystem, might be influenced by performance and not just dominance.
28	ICP	Internet Computer	Price has been volatile, dominance impact might be difficult to predict.
29	FTT	FTX Token	Native token of the FTX exchange, price might be influenced by performance and not just dominance.
30	XMR	Monero	Privacy-focused coin, price movements might not directly correlate with Bitcoin dominance.

Memecoins: The Wildcards

Memecoins, often driven by community support and viral marketing, add an unpredictable element to the cryptocurrency market. These coins, which started as jokes, have sometimes gained substantial value and market cap due to their popularity.

Dogecoin (DOGE)
Dogecoin, inspired by the popular "Doge" meme, began as a joke but quickly grew into a significant cryptocurrency. Its community is known for its charitable activities and tipping culture. Celebrity endorsements and social media trends have propelled Dogecoin to mainstream attention, making it a notable player in the crypto space.

Shiba Inu (SHIB)
Shiba Inu, dubbed the "Dogecoin killer," has gained a large following and significant market cap. Operating on the Ethereum blockchain, Shiba Inu leverages its community and viral marketing to drive interest and investment.

(There are an exhaustive list of thousands of Altcoin and memecoins, we only provide some examples here)

Strategic Implications for Investors

Understanding the interplay between Bitcoin dominance and altcoin performance is crucial for developing effective investment strategies. Here are some key takeaways:

Timing Market Entry and Exit: Monitoring Bitcoin dominance can help investors time their entry into or exit from altcoin positions. A declining dominance may signal an altseason, presenting opportunities to capitalize on rising altcoin prices.

Portfolio Diversification: Using Bitcoin dominance as a guide, investors can diversify their portfolios across multiple altcoins, reducing risk and maximizing potential returns.

Risk Management: Bitcoin dominance can serve as a risk management tool.

A sudden spike in dominance might indicate market stress, prompting a shift towards safer assets like Bitcoin.

List of Memecoins and examples of their correlation to bitcoin dominance

Rank	Symbol	Name	Reaction to Bitcoin Dominance
1	DOGE	Dogecoin	Memecoin with a passionate community, price can be more sentiment-driven than dominance-driven.
2	SHIB	Shiba Inu	Similar to DOGE, price is highly influenced by social media trends and hype.
3	FLOKI	Floki Inu	Another memecoin inspired by Elon Musk's dog, price movements can be erratic.
4	BABYDOGE	Baby Doge Coin	Yet another memecoin derivative, price can be extremely volatile.
5	SAMO	Samoyedcoin	Memecoin focused on promoting mental health awareness, price can be sentiment-driven.
6	Kishu Inu	Kishu Inu	Memecoin with a focus on building a decentralized ecosystem, price can be volatile.
7	BONK	Bonk	Memecoin associated with Solana, price can be influenced by both Solana ecosystem and meme trends.
8	BONE	Bone	Governance token for ShibaSwap, price might be more utility-driven than purely meme-based.
9	PEPE	PEPE	Memecoin featuring the Pepe the Frog meme, price movements can be unpredictable.
10	YOOSHI	YOOSHI	Memecoin inspired by the Yoshi character from Nintendo, price can be volatile.

11	PIT	Pitbull	Memecoin focused on dog rescue charities, price can be influenced by both meme trends and charitable efforts.
12	DOBO	DogeBonk	Combination of Dogecoin and Bonk memes, price can be highly speculative.
13	ELON	ELON	Memecoin inspired by Elon Musk, price movements can be erratic.
14	HOGE	Hoge Finance	Memecoin with a focus on DeFi integration, price might be influenced by both meme trends and DeFi adoption.
15	SAMOT	Samo Inu	Yet another memecoin inspired by the Samoyed dog breed, price can be volatile.
16	CATGIRL	Catgirl	Memecoin inspired by anime characters, price movements can be unpredictable.
17	WAGMI	WAGMI	Memecoin representing the phrase "We're All Gonna Make It," price can be sentiment-driven.
18	CUMMIES	CUMMIES	Memecoin with potentially NSFW (Not Safe For Work) associations
20	GRIM	Grim Finance	Governance token for a DeFi project, price is likely more driven by DeFi adoption than meme popularity.

Note: This list is not exhaustive and the price movements of memecoins can be highly volatile and unpredictable. They are often more influenced by social media trends and hype than by Bitcoin dominance or market fundamentals.

It's important to conduct your own research before investing in any memecoin.

Disclaimer: Due to the potentially NSFW nature of CUMMIES, it's important to exercise caution and conduct thorough research before considering any investment.

Chapter 10: Conclusion

As we reach the end of this comprehensive guide on understanding Bitcoin dominance and predicting altcoin bull runs, it's important to summarize the key insights and strategies that have been discussed.

The cryptocurrency market is a dynamic and rapidly evolving space, and staying informed about its trends and shifts is crucial for making informed investment decisions.
This chapter provides a concise review of the major points covered and offers some final thoughts on navigating the cryptocurrency landscape.

Summary of Key Takeaways
1. Demystifying Altcoins:

Altcoins, or alternative cryptocurrencies, offer a diverse range of functionalities and use cases beyond Bitcoin.

The innovation within the altcoin space drives the overall growth of the cryptocurrency market.
Understanding the different types of altcoins and their unique features is essential for building a diversified investment portfolio.
2. Understanding Bitcoin Dominance:

Bitcoin dominance is a key metric that measures Bitcoin's market cap relative to the total market cap of all cryptocurrencies.
Historical trends show that Bitcoin dominance fluctuates, impacting the performance of altcoins.
Monitoring Bitcoin dominance helps investors anticipate market shifts and adjust their strategies accordingly.
3. The Impact of Bitcoin Dominance on Altcoins:

Changes in Bitcoin dominance can significantly affect altcoin prices.
A decrease in Bitcoin dominance often signals an altcoin season, where altcoins outperform Bitcoin.

Understanding the correlation between Bitcoin and altcoin performance allows investors to make more informed decisions.

4. Key Indicators and Metrics:

Market cap, trading volume, liquidity, and network effects are crucial metrics for analyzing cryptocurrency investments.
Technical analysis tools and market sentiment indicators provide valuable insights for timing market entry and exit points.
Keeping an eye on these indicators helps investors navigate the volatile cryptocurrency market.

5. The Dance of Dominance: How Bitcoin Impacts Altcoin Seasons:

Altcoin seasons occur when altcoins outperform Bitcoin, usually during periods of declining Bitcoin dominance.
Historical examples, such as the 2017 and 2021 altseasons, highlight the cyclical nature of the market.

Identifying the onset of altcoin seasons involves monitoring Bitcoin dominance, trading volumes, and market sentiment.

6. Predicting Altcoin Bull Runs:

Predicting altcoin bull runs requires analyzing key signals like declining Bitcoin dominance, rising trading volumes, and positive market sentiment.

Tools such as CoinMarketCap, CoinGecko, TradingView, and sentiment analysis platforms help track market trends.
Case studies of successful predictions, like Ethereum and Binance Coin, provide practical insights for investors.

7. Investing Strategies for Altcoins:

Diversifying your portfolio across different altcoins minimizes risk and maximizes potential returns.
Timing investments based on Bitcoin dominance trends and using technical analysis to identify entry and exit points are crucial strategies.

Practical tips like conducting thorough research, staying updated with market trends, and using dollar-cost averaging enhance investment success.

8. The Future of Bitcoin and Altcoins:

Institutional adoption, technological advancements, DeFi growth, and integration with traditional finance are key trends shaping the future of cryptocurrencies.
Regulatory clarity and supportive frameworks will play a crucial role in fostering innovation and protecting investors.

Long-term predictions include Bitcoin solidifying its position as digital gold, altcoins driving innovation, and mainstream adoption accelerating.

Final Thoughts on Navigating the Crypto Market
The cryptocurrency market offers immense opportunities for investors, but it also comes with significant risks.

As with any investment, it is essential to conduct thorough research, stay informed about market developments, and adopt a strategic approach to managing your portfolio. Here are some final thoughts to keep in mind as you navigate the crypto market:

1. Stay Informed and Adaptable:
The cryptocurrency market is constantly evolving, with new technologies, regulations, and trends emerging regularly. Stay informed by following reputable news sources, engaging with the crypto community, and continuously learning about the latest developments. Being adaptable and open to change will help you navigate the market more effectively.

2. Manage Risks Wisely:
Risk management is crucial in the volatile world of cryptocurrencies. Diversify your portfolio, set stop-loss orders, and avoid investing more than you can afford to lose. By managing risks wisely, you can protect your investments and enhance your chances of long-term success.

3. Focus on Fundamentals:
While short-term price movements can be influenced by market sentiment and speculative trading, long-term success in the crypto market often depends on the fundamentals of the projects you invest in. Focus on altcoins with strong use cases, experienced teams, and robust technologies.

4. Embrace a Long-Term Perspective:
The cryptocurrency market can be highly volatile in the short term, but it has shown remarkable growth over the long term. Embrace a long-term perspective and avoid making impulsive decisions based on short-term market fluctuations. Patience and discipline are key to successful investing.

5. Continue Learning and Exploring:
The world of cryptocurrencies is vast and complex, with new innovations and opportunities constantly emerging. Continue learning and exploring different aspects of the market, from blockchain technology to decentralized finance and beyond.

By expanding your knowledge, you can uncover new investment opportunities and stay ahead of market trends.

Encouragement for Further Exploration

As you continue your journey in the world of cryptocurrencies, remember that this is an exciting and rapidly evolving field with endless possibilities. Whether you are a seasoned investor or a newcomer, there is always more to learn and explore. Embrace the challenges and opportunities that come your way, and stay curious and engaged with the crypto community.

The insights and strategies discussed in this book provide a solid foundation for understanding Bitcoin dominance and predicting altcoin bull runs. Use this knowledge to make informed investment decisions, manage risks, and capitalize on the dynamic shifts in the cryptocurrency market.

Appendices
Glossary of Key Terms:

Altcoin: Any cryptocurrency other than Bitcoin.
Bitcoin Dominance: The percentage of the total cryptocurrency market cap that is attributed to Bitcoin.
DeFi: Decentralized finance, financial services built on blockchain technology that operate without intermediaries.
Market Cap: The total value of a cryptocurrency, calculated by multiplying the current price by the total supply.
NFT: Non-fungible token, a unique digital asset representing ownership of a specific item or piece of content.

Additional Resources and Reading Materials:

CoinMarketCap: A leading platform for cryptocurrency market data and analysis.
CoinGecko: Another comprehensive source for cryptocurrency market data and insights.
TradingView: A platform for technical analysis and charting of various assets, including cryptocurrencies.
LunarCRUSH: A tool for sentiment analysis in the cryptocurrency market.
Author's Note and Contact Information:

As the author of this book, I hope you have found the information and insights provided to be valuable and enlightening. The cryptocurrency market is an exciting and dynamic space, and I encourage you to continue exploring and learning about its many facets. If you have any questions, feedback, or would like to connect, please feel free to reach out.

References:

Cited Works and Data Sources: Throughout this book, various sources of data and information have been referenced to provide accurate and up-to-date insights into the cryptocurrency market. These sources include market data platforms, industry reports, and academic research.

www.ingramcontent.com/pod-product-compliance
Lightning Source LLC
Chambersburg PA
CBHW031928240526
45464CB00023B/2186